THE GAY LIBERATION MOVEMENT

BEFORE AND AFTER STONEWALL

THE HISTORY OF THE LGBTQ+ RIGHTS MOVEMENT™

THE GAY LIBERATION MOVEMENT

BEFORE AND AFTER STONEWALL

SEAN HEATHER K. MCGRAW

Rosen
YA™
New York

Thank you to Robert and Nanci McGraw, brothers Darrin and Gavin, and for Cris, Q. B., and Gary

Published in 2019 by The Rosen Publishing Group, Inc.
29 East 21st Street, New York, NY 10010

Library of Congress Cataloging-in-Publication Data

Names: McGraw, Sean Heather K., author.
Title: The gay liberation movement : before and after Stonewall / Sean Heather K. McGraw.
Description: New York : Rosen Publishing, 2019. | Series: The history of the LGBTQ+ rights movement | Includes bibliographical references and index. | Audience: Grades 7–12.
Identifiers: LCCN 2017022203 | ISBN 9781538381342 (library bound) | ISBN 9781508183112 (pbk.)
Subjects: LCSH: Gay liberation movement—United States—History—Juvenile literature. | Gay rights—United States—History—Juvenile literature. | Stonewall Riots, New York, N.Y., 1969—Juvenile literature.
Classification: LCC HQ76.8.U5 M3949 2018 | DDC 323.3/2640973—dc23
LC record available at https://lccn.loc.gov/2017022203

Manufactured in the United States of America

On the cover: The raid on New York City's Stonewall Inn ignited riots on June 28, 1969 (*top*), and fueled a worldwide movement for gay rights and solidarity that would be seen in marches, such as this pride parade on Boston's Commonwealth Avenue in 1977 (*bottom*).

CONTENTS

INTRODUCTION

"Homosexuals are coming together at last," stated a flyer created by the Mattachine Society of New York. This flyer was given to people at a rally in New York City on Sunday, July 27, 1969, one month after the Stonewall riots of June 28, 1969. These words sum up the trajectory of the LGBTQ+ movement after the riots.

The Stonewall riots have served as a dividing line in the history of the LGBTQ+ movement, dividing history neatly into the before and after. Yet these words were written by members of the Mattachine Society, a group of gay men led by Harry Hay. In 1950, nineteen years before the Stonewall riots, Hay had established the society to educate mainstream society about matters to do with gay men. They had already come together before Stonewall, in groups, bars, and homes. And they had already had conflict with local authorities, such as during the Black Cat Tavern riot in 1967.

And yet something was different about Stonewall. Part of that difference is made clear by examining the years immediately before and after it, around 1965 to 1980. These years spanned the height of the African American civil rights movement; the anticapitalist antiwar movement that ended US involvement in the Vietnam War; the women's liberation movement, and the student and counterculture movements. The protest methods, rhetoric, and liberation ideology for these movements were similar. Each wanted civil rights to be more inclusive of previously excluded populations, and each included the participants

Seen here from left to right are Chuck Rowland, an unidentified man, Rudi Gernreich, Tony Reyes, and Don Slater. They were members of the Mattachine Society, the first American homophile group.

forming a core group identity for themselves. Each movement also built on the achievements and issues of the others. These years were crucial to the development of modern LGBTQ+ identity, culture, and legal status and have deeply influenced mainstream culture in many ways.

Many changes came about because of these events and the people involved in them. Along the way, there was much social and legal persecution against LGBTQ+ people. This persecution served as the basic "why" of the movement. People often hate what is different from them, and as a result persecution becomes enshrined for various reasons in culture, religion, and law. But no one likes to be bullied, and it is important to know what resistance looks like as well as what successes and failures result from that resistance.

While movements are a collective effort, they never involve fully uniform actors. LGBTQ+ people in particular are not and have never been a monolithic group. They are composed of many different types of people, with their own points of view that sometimes conflict.

Determining the events of history involves examining secondary sources written by expert scholars and news or media sources and interpreting the meaning of primary sources. Primary sources give us a better understanding of what occurred than secondary sources alone. However, all primary sources must still be interpreted with care because sometimes their information conflicts with other sources, is biased, or is unreliable in some other manner.

CHAPTER ONE

DENIAL AND ENTRAPMENT

T here was much social, legal, and medical discrimination against gay men and lesbians in the 1950s and 1960s. In reaction to those threats, gay men and lesbians established two major organizations to create safer communities for themselves in order to work toward being better accepted in society.

A HOSTILE COUNTRY

In 1965, the United States was undergoing great changes socially and politically. President Lyndon Baines Johnson proclaimed his vision of a "Great Society," in which education, medical care, and social welfare programs would be expanded and problems of urban and rural poverty and violence would be reduced. The Civil Rights Act of 1964 sought to end job discrimination and segregation for black Americans, and the Voting Rights Act of 1965 tried to assure voting rights for them. These laws proposed to remove unequal treatment among

President Lyndon B. Johnson signs the Civil Rights Act of 1964 to create a legal framework for outlawing employment, housing, and voting discrimination based on race, color, sex, national origin, and religion.

blacks and whites and reduce discrimination against other nationalities or ethnic minority groups. For many, it seemed that society would become better for African Americans, Hispanics, and other minorities. At the same time, tolerance on a social level was hard won. For example, white supremacists hindered the Selma to Montgomery march that Martin Luther King Jr. led, and riots in the Watts neighborhood in Los Angeles were sparked by a violent arrest after a long period of discriminatory policing.

The Vietnam War was escalating on both sides, and the number of American troops on the ground was increasing. In response, the group Students for

Betty Friedan (*far left*) and other notable women, including Rosalynn Carter and Betty Ford (*third and fourth from left*), rallied for the Equal Rights Amendment at the 1977 National Women's Conference in Houston, Texas.

a Democratic Society managed to get more than twenty-five thousand protesters to fill the streets of Washington, DC, in response.

In 1966, the National Organization for Women was founded by prominent leaders such as Betty Friedan, Shirley Chisholm, and Muriel Fox. The resistance of the civil rights movement helped inspire the anti–Vietnam War movement and the women's liberation movement.

ANTIGAY SENTIMENTS AND POLICY

For queer people, life was full of discrimination because they lacked certain legal rights. They could be fired at any time by their employer and denied service in retail establishments, refused work, and denied access to health care. The ability to adopt children, marry, have domestic unions, or serve openly in the military was also not legal or allowed for them. They were often excluded from churches, holding church and government positions, and social clubs. Cross-dressers, then called transvestites, were also discriminated against in this manner.

The reason they were so shunned is that mainstream society viewed them as deviants, both socially and psychologically. Fictional works exposed the attitudes people had toward the existence of homosexuality. A 1959 lesbian pulp fiction novel, *Private School*, written by J. G. Priest, had this announcement on its front cover: "Every parent should read this shocking novel of adolescent girls who first tolerated vice—then embraced it—then could not live without it!" The cover of another pulp fiction book, *Edge of Twilight,* by Paula Christian, called same-sex love "that outcast world of 'twilight' love." The cover of *The Third Sex*, by Artemis Smith, stated, "Here is a penetrating study of society's greatest curse: homosexuality!" Homosexuality was commonly called "the love that dare not speak its name," which indicates a general uneasiness to even openly talk about it or admit that it existed.

While civil life was already difficult, the law and medical institutions made life much harder for LGBTQ+ people, specifically those labeled as "homosexuals" or "transvestites." Whether or not a person labeled as such was actually gay didn't matter to those who "treated" or imprisoned them. There were laws in every state called sodomy laws that made sexual acts between same-sex couples punishable by fines and/or imprisonment. In conjunction with these laws, serious works of science reflected an intolerant attitude toward LGBTQ+ people and prescribed a solution for dealing with them. Such publications legitimized medical professionals treating that minority horribly. *The Diagnostic and Statistical Manual* (*DSM-I*), in particular, used the word "homosexual" as a medical term, thereby labeling homosexuality as a type of illness. The word was actually coined by Austrian writer Karl-Maria Kertbeny, himself a gay man who opposed sodomy laws.

What the world wanted of LGBTQ+ people was for them to become heterosexual and gender normative. Doctors and laymen alike regarded homosexuality and transvestitism as mental disorders, ones that were somehow contagious to others. Medical and psychiatric opinion was that people with such identities were violent sex offenders. The medical establishment thought that gay people in particular were unable to control their sexual desires and that they were "sexual psychopaths." They, along with transvestites, were viewed as criminals who needed to be rounded up and put in a psychiatric ward or prison until cured. In fact, in the 1930s, New York City special deputy police commissioner Carleton Simon and

Seen here from left to right are William B. Bradley, Arthur Miller, Reverend L. Sylvester Odom, and Rabbi Samuel Adelman.

Congressman Arthur L. Miller were among influential officials who thought that the best way to deal with homosexuals should be to attempt to cure them of homosexuality. Doctors recommended conversion therapy, and since various psychiatrists and those associated with them wrote the *DSM-I*, that book also offered at least implicit justification for using conversion therapy. Miller was the author of legislation, which he referred to as a "sex pervert bill," that made sodomy punishable by up to twenty years in prison. Drugs, chemical castration, and antipsychotic medicine were routinely administered to homosexual patients.

WHAT DO THESE WORDS MEAN?

The names used to describe nonheteronormative attraction changed dramatically in the nineteenth and twentieth centuries. Karl-Maria Kertbeny, an Austrian journalist, first used the terms "homosexual" and "heterosexual" in 1869. By the early twentieth century, "homosexual" and "heterosexual" had become the preferred terms used by the scientific community.

Many LGBTQ+ people used the term "homosexual" to describe themselves, although other terms existed, such as "invert" in Britain and "Urning," for a gay man, in Germany. "Homosexual" was primarily used for men but gradually also included women, just as the term "mankind" means "all men and women." By the second decade of the twentieth century, "gay" acquired the meaning of "same-sex attracted person," a meaning that gained more popularity in the 1960s. But its original meaning is "happy" or "carefree." Gay often refers to men, but it can refer to either sex. Similarly, the term "lesbian," which describes only same-sex attracted women, has been in use since the mid-nineteenth century, alongside its earlier meaning, "a person or export from the Greek isle of Lesbos."

"Transgender" is an umbrella term describing someone whose gender identity doesn't match the sex they were assigned at birth. "Transsexual" was used to describe a transgender person who desires to undergo or has completed transition, a process that involves causing the body to match one's gender identity. The term "transgender" is now more commonly used to describe those who undergo a medical gender transition and those who do not. Virginia Prince, a transgender woman who coined the word "transgenderal" in 1965, used the word to describe gender identity on strictly psychological terms. According to Prince, gender had nothing to do with genitalia but was more psychosocial in nature.

"Queer" is an umbrella term that describes being either non-heteronormative, non-gender normative, or both. It was originally used as a pejorative term, but LGBTQ+ communities have reclaimed it.

THE MATTACHINE SOCIETY AND THE DAUGHTERS OF BILITIS

Some gay people began to organize in response to their need to survive in a hostile world. Harry Hay and others established the Mattachine Society in 1950 to protest the firing of alleged homosexuals in the US government, which continued throughout the 1950s and 1960s. Once fired or arrested, these people had no paths for legal redress. Men and women often could not get another job, and divorces and suicides were common.

The Mattachine Society originally was a secret society because of the risk of being exposed in the

This is a portrait of Harold L. "Hal" Call from 1953. He became the president of the Mattachine Society that year.

McCarthy era. Under McCarthyism, communists and homosexuals were treated as the greatest enemies of the nation. Hal Call, who was elected the society's president in 1953, was determined to make it a public organization. His goal was to make the society more visible and to be able to work with local experts to further research and gain professional expertise in homosexuality.

The Daughters of Bilitis (DOB), founded in San Francisco by the couple Phyllis Lyon and Del Martin and others in 1955, sought to be a social group for lesbians and to promote tolerance in mainstream society for them. Martin and Lyon's home soon became a lesbian community center. It wasn't long before they published a newsletter, *The Ladder*, to proclaim their mission to increase tolerance of lesbians.

These organizations and others like them around the world were called homophile movements. The word "homophile," which first appeared in a 1924 doctoral thesis written by the German psychologist Karl-Günther Heimsoth, and came from the Greek words for "same" and "love" to emphasize an emotional connection between people and not simply sexual activities. These homophile organizations expressed that people who actually were homosexuals should be discreet and that they should work to prove to mainstream society that they were not promiscuous, violent, or pedophiles. They sent out newsletters, spoke with psychologists, and organized peaceful protests. However, neither of these organizations had many people in them, and they often served the needs of middle-class men and women instead of working-class people.

GAY BAR RAIDS

Many working-class queers found that bars were one of the few places they could be even somewhat open about who they were. There were middle-class men and women in these establishments, too, but these bars were often dingy and located in rough neighborhoods. There were also specific lesbian bars, like Rusty's in Philadelphia, as well as coed bars, like the Black Cat.

Many states did not allow bars to cater their services, specifically alcoholic drinks, to queers at gay bars. So-called gay bars generally strived to serve people across the entire LGBTQ+ spectrum, not just gay men. Men, especially, though, were routinely picked up in bars and parks for vagrancy and lewdness charges, and bars were commonly raided. These raids involved arresting people, revoking liquor licenses, and shutting down the entire bar. The New York State Liquor Authority sought control over queer people's access to liquor and thus the ability to congregate with other queer people. Often it was only bars that were owned and run by the Mafia that would defy these laws and serve queer people, and even though the Mafia paid the cops to allow them to stay open, police raids were still commonplace.

While more men than women tended to be arrested, women were not exempt from arrest and prosecution. Effeminate men, who were called queens, drag queens, and cross-dressers, and masculine women, called butches, were especially targeted, but even femmes whose dress habits matched what was typical of their sex were arrested. One Mattachine member, Jim Kepner, stated, "Bars [were] raided. Guys murdered by someone they had picked up or someone saw them on the street and thought they were queer. Public officials [were] arrested in public tearooms." Hal Call, executive director of the Mattachine Society said,

"Back in the 1960s, the police were playing cat and mouse with the guys, not the women. The male homosexual was a threat to the straight man. That's where the problem was. Females didn't count. [...] The cops could do anything they wanted. All we could do was run and hide."

But lesbians *did* count; their bars were not exempt. In Philadelphia, on a night in March 1968, policemen raided the lesbian bar Rusty's. They kicked out the owner of the bar, Rusty Parisi, and arrested at least ten lesbians.

CHAPTER TWO

COMPTON'S, BLACK CAT, AND STONEWALL

O utside of the new organizations that advocated for LGBTQ+ rights, there would be incidents that offered the chance for gays and lesbians to fight for their civil rights, and these would serve as a reminder of the fact that their freedom and well-being were always at stake. Many sources describe the riots and the police response to the resistance they faced. Newspapers published at the time also shed some light on the Stonewall riots, in particular, although they were usually unaccepting of queer identities. If anything, hostile sources at least serve as corroboration that some significant event took place.

THE COMPTON'S CAFETERIA RIOT AND THE BLACK CAT TAVERN

LGBTQ+ people caught up in raids did not always run and hide. The locals who frequented Gene Compton's cafeteria on Turk and Taylor Streets in San Francisco's seedy Tenderloin district were street kids, hustlers, drag queens, and others considered undesirable by mainstream society. One late August night in 1966 at Gene Compton's cafeteria, those customers met the usual police cleanup with defiance. It all started to go down when a drag queen threw coffee at an officer.

By the end of the night, rioters broke windows and dishes and burned a nearby newsstand. The management opened on the next day but decided to refuse entry to drag queens. Then came the Vanguard, a group of young gay street hustlers, teens, and queens. The group had been founded at the nearby Glide Memorial Methodist Church, which progressively sought to provide spaces for disadvantaged gay youth. They had a logo and a mission statement that read in part: "Vanguard is an organization for the youth in the Tenderloin attempting to get its citizens a sense of dignity and responsibility too long denied." The Vanguard protested the day after Compton's Cafeteria denied entry to drag queens.

At the Black Cat Tavern in Los Angeles, when policemen started their customary raid in the early hours of January 1, 1967, patrons fought back unsuccessfully. It was a bloody affair, and policemen smashed glasses and beat up several people. Robert Haas, the bartender, endured a ruptured spleen. Sixteen people were arrested and told to lie down on the sidewalk.

The next day, Steve Ginsburg's small group, Personal Rights in Defense and Education (PRIDE), protested with leaflets and banners

GENE COMPTON'S
CAFETERIA RIOT 1966

HERE MARKS THE SITE OF GENE
COMPTON'S CAFETERIA WHERE A RIOT
TOOK PLACE ONE AUGUST NIGHT WHEN
TRANSGENDER WOMEN AND GAY MEN
STOOD UP FOR THEIR RIGHTS AND FOUGHT
AGAINST POLICE BRUTALITY, POVERTY
OPPRESSION AND DISCRIMINATION
IN THE TENDERLOIN.
WE, THE TRANSGENDER, GAY, LESBIAN AND
BISEXUAL COMMUNITY, ARE DEDICATING
THIS PLAQUE TO THESE HEROES OF
OUR CIVIL RIGHTS MOVEMENT

DEDICATED JUNE 22, 2006

This plaque in the Tenderloin district of San Francisco commemorates the August 1966 riot between police and gay and drag queen customers at Gene Compton's cafeteria.

that proclaimed that there should be "No More Abuse of Our Rights and Dignity." These riots were prominent within the LGBTQ+ community, particularly in California, but they have not captured the historical attention of the Stonewall riots. It therefore wasn't until the Stonewall riots that many disparate groups would be galvanized to use more militant tactics and demand that mainstream society accept them completely.

THE STONEWALL RIOTS: QUEENS AND BUTCHES

Like many other gay bars, the Stonewall Inn was owned by Mafia families who paid off the police to leave them alone. However, this didn't mean that the police wouldn't raid the bars. The police thought they were going to have an easy time in their customary practice of raiding on June 28, 1969, at the Stonewall Inn. The Stonewall usually served young effeminate gay men, drag queens, leather men, butch and femme working-class lesbians, blacks, whites, Latinos, and Asians.

When the police came into the bar, the first thing they did was round up the patrons and escort them outside. They began to put patrons in paddy wagons and note their names and identification. The police took the proceeds from the cash register to investigate whether that money consisted of illegal funds.

The raid was the third police raid on the bar that week, but this time, the two hundred patrons didn't simply disperse. A crowd gathered outside and began to hum with fervor as they observed the patrons being roughly manhandled and arrested. An article written a few days later by Jeffrey Lisker for the *New York Daily News* stated that as the police did

Vito Genovese (*left*) is seen here entering a courthouse in 1959. He was the leader of the Genovese crime family that helped open the Stonewall Inn in 1967.

what they thought was routine work, the mood of the crowd began to change. He wrote:

> *Only a handful of police were on hand...They ushered the patrons out onto Christopher Street, just off Sheridan Square. A crowd had formed in front of the Stonewall and the customers were greeted with cheers of encouragement from the gallery. The whole proceeding took on the aura of a homosexual Academy Awards Night. The Queens pranced out to the street blowing kisses and waving to the crowd.*

But this encouragement by the crowd and the general feeling of curiosity and carnivalesque behaviors soon transformed into a much louder and more violent response. Several eyewitnesses noted that a butch lesbian was handcuffed and hauled out of the bar by police into a patrol car, but she several times got out of the other side of the car. Finally, as a police officer wrestled her, she yelled, "Why don't you do something?" Lisker wrote what eyewitnesses had seen:

> *Then, without warning, Queen Power exploded with all the fury of a gay atomic bomb. Queens, princesses and ladies-in-waiting began hurling anything they could get their polished, manicured fingernails on. Bobby pins, compacts, curlers, lipstick tubes and*

other femme fatale missiles were flying in the direction of the cops. The war was on. The lilies of the valley had become carnivorous jungle plants. Urged on by cries of "C'mon girls, lets go get 'em," the defenders of Stonewall launched an attack.

POLICE RESPONSE AND COUNTERRESPONSE

Lisker's account continues, "The cops called for assistance. To the rescue came the Tactical Patrol Force." The crowd threw bottles, bricks, anything they could get their hands on, and they set fires and wrote graffiti such as "legalize gay bars" and "support gay power."

A witness, Morty Manford, stated,

Then someone apparently threw a rock, which broke one of the windows on the second floor. [...] A few more rocks went flying and then somebody from inside the bar opened the door and stuck out a gun. He yelled for people to stay back. Then he withdrew the gun, closed the door, and went back inside. Somebody took an uprooted parking meter and broke the glass in the front window and the plywood board that was behind it. One way or another, though, gay people had stood up and rebelled.

Two people in particular, Marsha P. Johnson and Rey "Sylvia Lee" Rivera, both drag queens, were important players in the drama of the Stonewall riots. Several witnesses have confirmed that Johnson was one of the first participants to throw a brick and other objects at the police, reportedly shimmying up a telephone pole for a better vantage point.

Rivera also has stated that she was one of the first participants in the riots. In a 1989 interview, she offered the following account:

> I just happened to be there when it all jumped off. The Stonewall wasn't a bar for drag queens... And only a certain number of drag queens were allowed into the Stonewall at that time...Suddenly, the nickels, dimes, pennies, and quarters started flying. I threw quarters and pennies and whatnot...The cops locked themselves into the bar. It was getting vicious. Then someone set fire to the Stonewall...How long can you live in the closet like that?...I didn't really get hurt...But I saw other people being hurt by the police. There was one drag queen, I don't know what she said, but they just beat her into a bloody pulp. There were a couple of dykes they took out and threw in a car. The dykes got out the other side.

INTERPRETATIONS OF THE STONEWALL RIOTS

In subsequent years, the stories of what happened that night have conflicted. The discordant memories and portrayals primarily hinge on the races, classes, and genders of the participants. Rivera remembered that the bar was not a place where drag queens were especially welcome, but all witnesses say that they were there nevertheless. Rivera remembered the presence of some lesbians, particularly working-class butches and femmes, but how many there were is still debated. Other witnesses focus on the strong presence of the lesbians that were there fighting back against the police. How many effeminate gay men and others were there is also debated, as is the racial component of the participants.

One thing that does seem to be agreed upon is the large presence of usually effeminate and often homeless gay street youth. The primary documents available are sparse, and there is one photograph available that shows white, effeminate gay men, most likely street youth, struggling with the police.

One of the problematic issues in the memories of the Stonewall riots is the conflicting reports of who, specifically, was there. Marsha P. Johnson indicated that she didn't remember Sylvia Rivera being there on the first night, implying that she was there on the second night but not the first. And another participant, Doric Wilson, stated emphatically that Rivera was not

(continued on the next page)

(continued from the previous page)

SUNDAY, JUNE 29, 1969 / Partly sunny   Weather: page 16

Village Raid Stirs Melee

A police raid in the Stonewall Inn, a tavern frequented by homosexuals at 53 Christopher St., just east of Sheridan Square in Greenwich Village, triggered a near riot early today. As persons seized in the raid were driven away by police, hundreds of passerby's shouting "Gay Power" and "We Want Freedom" laid siege to the tavern with an improvised battering ram, garbage cans, bottles and beer cans in a project demonstration.

Police reinforcements were rushed to the tavern to deal with the disturbances, which continued for more that two hours. By the time calm returned to the area at least 12 persons had been arrested on charges ranging from assault to disorderly conduct. Among those arrested was fold singer Dave Van Ronk, 33, of 15 Sheridan Sq., who was charged with felonious assault on a police officer. Van Ronk was not in the tavern, but got into the fight when it spilled out onto the street, police said. Police said the raid was staged because of unlicensed sale of liquor on the premises.

This June 29, 1969, *New York Post* article by Luis Torres described the events at the Stonewall of the previous night.

there. Rivera's statements though, even if not factually true for Rivera, do seem to indicate the larger truths of the riots. Drag queens were beaten; people did throw objects; and there were lesbians and street youths, queens, and black, white, and Hispanic people. Whatever the truth of Rivera's participation, the Stonewall riots have been portrayed often and have come to occupy an iconic place in the history of the gay liberation movement.

THE RIOT THAT KEPT GOING

The riot lasted into the early hours of the morning. The police were astonished at the response and barricaded themselves in the bar. One officer stated that he was injured when a can was thrown at him. All in all, four officers were injured in the riot. "They were throwing more than lace hankies," one inspector said. "I was almost decapitated by a slab of thick glass. It was thrown like a discus and just missed my throat by inches. The beer can didn't miss, though, it hit me right above the temple."

Four days after the first Stonewall incident, on July 2, 1969, a group gathered in front of the bar to see if it was operating as usual and to see if the police would harass them.

The next night, people began to riot again while the Stonewall Inn was shuttered and damaged. Hundreds of people gathered to participate and reenact the violent demonstrations that had occurred the first night. Just as before, the tactical riot police were called out and people on both sides were injured.

On the following Monday and Tuesday night, everyone spontaneously rested, but on Wednesday night a violent riot erupted. That would be the end of the resistance at the Stonewall Inn.

While homophile movements had made great strides in getting acceptance and certain policies have changed for many gay people, the militancy and tactics that the Stonewall riots ushered in forever changed the ways in which they, as well as others across the LGBTQ+ spectrum, thought of themselves and the ways in which they sought solutions against discrimination. The hallmark slogans of the movement would now be "Gay Is Good!" And "Gay Power!"

CHAPTER THREE

AFTER STONEWALL

In the immediate aftermath of the Stonewall riots, a rally and march were organized by New York City gay men and lesbians to keep the spirit of the riots alive. New organizations emerged—secular and religious—as well as an annual Stonewall riots commemorative march in New York City and Los Angeles.

MEETING HATE HEAD-ON

A flyer handed out shortly after the riots by the members of Craig Rodwell's Homophile Youth Movement in Neighborhoods (HYMN) diagnosed the reason why police had targeted the Stonewall Inn:

> *The nights of Friday, June 27, 1969 and Saturday, June 28, 1969 will go down in history as the first time that thousands of Homosexual men and women went out into the streets to protest the intolerable situation which has existed in New York City for many*

years—namely, the Mafia (or syndicate) control of this city's Gay bars in collusion with certain elements in the Police Dept. of the City of New York. The demonstrations were triggered by a Police raid on the Stonewall Inn late Friday night, June 27th. The purported reason for the raid was the Stonewall's lack of a liquor license. Who's kidding whom here? Can anybody really believe that an operation as big as the Stonewall could continue for almost three years just a few blocks from the 6th Precinct house without having a liquor license? No! The Police have known about the Stonewall operation all along. What's

On July 2, 1969, the gay community gathered on Christopher Street to continue to protest police harassment.

happened is the presence of new "brass" in 6th Precinct which has vowed to "drive the fags out of the Village."

It was plain and simple to the observers and participants that the police wanted to get rid of the queer presence in the area, even if the observers, in this instance, only seemed to acknowledge the threat as being directed toward gay people. It is unclear what sparked the spontaneous decision to protest the police treatment of gays, but frustration at their outcast status as well as exhaustion from the constant need to protect themselves probably were major factors. In addition, the militancy of the 1960s in the African American civil rights and antiwar movements probably encouraged people to engage in resistance.

If the resistance had ended with those riots, though, it would not have been a long-lived victory for the LGBTQ+ community.

A MARCH TOWARD THE GAY LIBERATION FRONT

Queer people around the country became even more politicized and began to mobilize and organize. The LGBTQ+ community decided to openly challenge and change social and legal proscriptions against those collectively labeled "homosexuals" and to increase their own self-awareness and self-esteem. Borrowing from the young women's liberation movement, a group of dissatisfied men

Even though the Gay Liberation Front (GLF) was formed in New York City, it quickly spread to Great Britain. Here a member shows a newsletter, *Come Together*, announcing a Gay Day for August 1971.

and women met on July 24, 1969, and formed the Gay Liberation Front (GLF).

After this first meeting, another meeting was held at a local leftist center, called Alternate U. In July 1969, one month after Stonewall, members of the GLF held a rally to commemorate the events, with Martha Shelley and Marty Robinson being the main speakers. Martha Shelley remembered its inception:

Mattachine was already having a meeting about the riots and all these gays showed up at the meeting to talk about what was going on. I showed up with a proposal for a jointly sponsored march. Dick Leitsch, who was the head of Mattachine, wasn't really into it, but when he asked for a vote—"How many people are in favor of holding a march?"—every hand went up.

In August 1969, the members protested at an antiwar rally in Central Park and brought a banner saying, "Gay Liberation Front." These protestors sought to distance themselves from the rhetoric of the Mattachine Society and the Daughters of Bilitis while building on their organizational heritage. The GLF began to organize consciousness-raising groups, study groups, and women's and men's groups and to seek the widest audiences possible for their message. They adopted Frank Kameny's statement that "Gay Is Good" and the phrase "Gay Power."

Soon, GLF chapters arose in cities across the United States. Gary Pavlic, of Albany, New York, remembered:

It might have been a week or two later, we had one of the drag queens who was involved in Stonewall come up and speak to us. That was really the beginning of the community here in Albany...We met at the Chapel— cultural center downtown...that was the first time I had ever publicly been able to admit that I was gay.

STONEWALL IN FILM

Stonewall has been portrayed in several dramatic films and documentaries, and it has been written about by many scholars and activists. All of them have received criticism of their portrayal of what happened and who was doing what.

The most recent film, *Stonewall* (2015), has been criticized because it portrays a young white man as one of the leaders of the riots, seen yelling "gay power" and throwing rocks. The film has been criticized for not portraying the nonwhite drag queens who participated in a more prominent and serious manner. In addition, critics have stated that the importance of lesbians in the riots and the galvanized movement afterward were almost entirely ignored or their importance greatly understated. However, the film does portray the main character becoming a gay street hustler, which was a group traditionally attendant at many gay bars.

The documentary *Stonewall Uprising* (2010), based on the nonfiction book by David Carter called *Stonewall: The Riots That Sparked the Gay Revolution*, includes eyewitness accounts from police as well as participants and interviews with a number of activists and participants in the riots and the immediate aftermath, such as Officer Seymour Pine, protest march coordinator and founder of the Gay Liberation Front Martha Shelley, coparticipant Doric Wilson, reporter Howard Smith, and others.

This meeting led over a dozen men to found the Gay Liberation Front of Albany and subsequently, Pavlic and a dozen other men founded the Gay Community Center, now called the Pride Center of Albany.

COMMEMORATION AND RELIGIOUS ACCEPTANCE

Craig Rodwell, the founder of HYMN and the Oscar Wilde Bookstore (the first gay bookstore in New York City), along with Linda Rhodes and Ellen Broidy, wrote a resolution to the Eastern Regional Conference of Homophile Organizations (ERCHO) to recommend an annual commemorative Christopher Street

On June 28, 1970, a year after the Stonewall riots, thousands of gay men and lesbians marched in Central Park in New York City to commemorate the riots and advocate for gay liberation.

Liberation Day. Another person who called for such an event was Brenda Howard. She suggested organizing an annual march and other weeklong commemorative events. She and L. Craig Schoonmaker began the practice of calling it a "Pride Parade."

In San Francisco, a small number of people marched in the 1970 Freedom Day Celebration. In 1972, thousands of people came to "Christopher Street West" in San Francisco, and this started an annual tradition that is still one of the largest crowd gatherings worldwide.

The Stonewall wasn't the only bar raided in the country. A year earlier, in 1968, a police raid at a Los Angeles bar, the Patch, inspired Pentecostal reverend Troy Perry to do something. He had talked to one person about the raid who had commented

Reverend Troy Perry (*center*), founder of the Metropolitan Community Church (MCC), officiates at this wedding ceremony for Rejean Tremblay (*left*) and Michel Girouard (*right*).

that he felt that God had abandoned gay people. Perry himself had been expelled from his original congregation for being gay, and he came to see that gay people needed to feel welcomed by religion and that they needed access to spirituality and to a god who loved them.

In October 1968, Reverend Perry had taken out an ad, and twelve men and women came to his home to attend the first service of what would come to be known as the Metropolitan Community Church (MCC). Rapidly, more and more people attended. Most were gay men and lesbians who longed for a religious house of worship that wouldn't ostracize them and tell them that they were damned. Perry said, "Gay people came to our church out of the shadows, out of the closets, out of the half-world."

After Stonewall, more and more gay men and lesbians felt encouraged to come out of the closet and renew their spirituality, which for many had been jettisoned for years because of religious discrimination against them. By 1972, Perry bought a building, and in 1973, more than a thousand people attended his services.

Perry's church was persecuted by homophobic people, and at one point, the building was set on fire. Perry's church was a Pentecostal conservative church in its liturgy but welcoming to all LGBTQ+ people, even allowing Wiccan practitioners and Jewish gay people space to practice their beliefs. Jewish gay men and lesbians were eventually encouraged to form their own temple within MCC's building.

Perry also joined the GLF and became a valuable ally. In Los Angeles in June 1970, GLF leaders Morris Kight, Perry, and Reverend Bob Humphries sponsored another Christopher Street West commemorative parade. They had trouble getting a permit from the police to march, but a California Supreme Court decision allowed the march to continue without the excessive $1 million charge. From Perry's efforts and the encouragement of others, several denominations were formed to cater to gay men and lesbians, and several denominations, particularly many Protestant and Jewish groups, have made great strides in accepting LGBTQ+ people.

CHAPTER FOUR

MISOGYNY CAUSES ORGANIZATIONS TO RESTRUCTURE

● ●

There was much disunity and dissension within the LGBTQ+ community in the 1970s. This was clear from the changing makeup of the organizing landscape, as some groups didn't survive the conflict. Further, while natural allies in some respects, gay men, lesbians, and transgender people had and still have different experiences and different needs. Each group began to organize around its own needs and experiences while also being part of the larger liberation movement.

GAY ACTIVISTS ALLIANCE AND ITS "ZAPS"

One characteristic of the organizing process in the 1970s was that people differed with each other about strategies and goals for achieving gay liberation. The formation of splinter groups was a constant pattern. These organizations were democratic and consensus driven, but because there were many different opinions among them, they were not particularly long-lived.

This photo depicts one of the many zaps of the Gay Activists Alliance (GAA) in 1975. These activists are protesting a television episode that the GAA thought gave prejudicial advice to gay men.

The Gay Liberation Front lasted until 1972. But the GLF paved the way for many other organizations to follow suit. The founders of GLF, Marty Robinson, Martha Shelley, and others, were unhappy with the unorganized and amorphous style of the GLF. The Gay Activists Alliance (GAA) branched off from the Gay Liberation Front in December 1969 because several members decided they did not like the practice of giving money to other causes, such as the Black Panthers.

GLF treasurer Jim Owles, GLF founders Lois Hart and Marty Robinson, and some others founded the GAA to achieve rights for gay people. The members of the GAA felt that while other causes were good, achieving gay rights and using confrontational tactics should be their focus.

The GAA led many "zaps," confrontational exercises to gain recognition and change public policies. Members infiltrated Radio City Music Hall while Mayor John Lindsay was speaking and yelled that he should sponsor a nondiscrimination order for the city. Eventually after many zaps, Lindsay ordered that the NYC Civil Service Commission not discriminate against gay people in hiring. It was a small, but significant, victory.

In Los Angeles, members of the Gay Liberation Front did their own zaps. Their most famous stunt was publicly pretending that they were going to colonize Alpine, a remote California town, and make it a gay-only area. News broadcasters and the three hundred or so residents of Alpine did not relish that possibility.

LESBIAN FEMINISM

The gay and lesbian community, itself, was as much affected by principles of division as of unity.

Throughout the 1970s and into the 1980s, the gay liberation movement was impacted by tension between lesbians and gay men. Though lesbians and bisexual women were involved in the Stonewall riots, in the early parades, the GLF and GAA, and legal and social civil rights actions, women often felt that men either ignored them or expected them to be homemakers for the movement who wouldn't be allowed to make any decisions. Women also felt that gay men were in general just as misogynistic as heterosexual men. Some gay men who were involved in different groups have admitted that there was in general a pervasive misogyny. Consequently, many women avoided the organizations and social spaces where men typically congregated and branched off to form their own.

Lesbians would soon begin to organize around feminism. Some felt that men (gay and straight) discriminated against them for being women and for being lesbians, so they wished to separate themselves as much as possible from all men. One such group splintered off from the Gay Liberation Front and the Gay Activists Alliance. It began when Jean O'Leary, a former nun, decided in 1969 that she would form a subcommittee of GAA called the Lesbian Liberation Committee. Between 1973 and 1974, the group was renamed Lesbian Feminist Liberation (LFL) (it was sometimes informally called the Lesbians for Liberation), and chapters were created in many different cities. LFL sought to create a space where lesbian and

In 2011, Ivy Bottini was recognized for her achievements by the city of Los Angeles, California. Some of those achievements include cofounding NOW and many years of activism on lesbian issues.

women's issues would be paramount. It was meant to offer a space of refuge from mainstream patriarchal society.

The creation of this organization coincided with the growing second-wave feminist movement that had begun in the early 1960s. Most notable was the 1966 formation of the National Organization for Women (NOW), begun by Betty Friedan, Ivy Bottini, and others. It was Bottini, a lesbian, who had created the NOW logo and urged that the issues of lesbians be prioritized, but Friedan and others felt that lesbians were a "lavender menace" that would detract from the feminist mission of achieving legal and social equality with men.

Bottini and other lesbians began to create lesbian feminism, a feminism focused on lesbians and their needs. At the 1970 NOW annual conference, the Radicalesbians, a group of lesbians who had also been GLF members, marched up to the podium. Among their ranks were Rita Mae Brown, Lois Hart, and Ellen Bedoz. They read their manifesto, "The Woman-Identified Woman." In this manifesto, they outlined their belief that all women needed to become lesbians (i.e. woman-identified women, not man-identified women); that men had always oppressed women; and that if women continued to focus on men's needs to the exclusion of women's needs, women would never overcome patriarchal oppression. NOW responded by opening the group to lesbians and actively seeking their input in feminist matters.

EXCERPT: "THE WOMAN-IDENTIFIED WOMAN"

The following passage was taken from a 1970 manifesto written by a collective known as the Radicalesbians. It sums up their evaluation of male chauvinism as a means of policing the roles, and by extension, the ambitions of women:

The grudging admiration felt for the tomboy, and the queasiness felt around a sissy boy point to the same thing: the contempt in which women—or those who play a female role—are held. And the investment in keeping women in that contemptuous role is very great. Lesbian is a word, the label, the condition that holds women in line. When a woman hears this word tossed her way, she knows she is stepping out of line. She knows that she has crossed the terrible boundary of her sex role. She recoils, she protests, she reshapes her actions to gain approval. Lesbian is a label invented by the Man to throw at any woman who dares to be his equal, who dares to challenge his prerogatives (including that of all women as part of the exchange medium among men), who dares to assert the primacy of her own needs.

LESBIAN SEPARATISM

Beginning in 1970, a growing number of lesbians sought to create independent spaces for lesbians, where their culture might flourish and their needs would be acknowledged and met. Beginning in 1973 with Barbara Grier's Naiad Press, women began creating publishing companies to publish lesbian-themed books. Many authors published books, essays, fiction and nonfiction, poetry, and prose, such as

Audre Lorde taught writing and feminism during her 1983 writer's residency at the Atlantic Center for the Arts in New Smyrna Beach, Florida.

Rubyfruit Jungle (1973) by Rita Mae Brown, *Diving into the Wreck* (1973) by Adrienne Rich, *Coal* (1976) by Audre Lorde, *The Lesbian Body* (1973) by Monique Wittig, *The Female Man* (1975) by Joanna Russ, and *Happy Endings Are All Alike* (1978) by Sandra Scoppettone.

EXCERPT: BLACK FEMINISM—COMBAHEE RIVER COLLECTIVE STATEMENT

One common critique of second-wave feminism is that it failed to include people of color. Even so, people of color have made space for themselves within the women's liberation movement. The passage below discusses the need to expand the language and tactics of feminism to recognize the intersectionality of systems of oppression in order to create a more effective resistance:

"We are a collective of Black feminists who have been meeting together since 1974... The most general statement of our politics at the present time would be that we are actively committed to struggling against racial, sexual, heterosexual, and class oppression, and see as our particular task the development of integrated analysis and practice based upon the fact that the major systems of oppression are

interlocking. The synthesis of these oppressions creates the conditions of our lives. As Black women we see Black feminism as the logical political movement to combat the manifold and simultaneous oppressions that all women of color face...We believe that sexual politics under patriarchy is as pervasive in Black women's lives as are the politics of class and race. We also often find it difficult to separate race from class from sex oppression because in our lives they are most often experienced simultaneously."

In addition, lesbians began to create lesbian-focused music and music festivals geared toward allowing lesbians to celebrate their sexual identity and meet other lesbians. The Michigan Womyn's Festival, which began in August 1976 and had its last installment in 2015, became the largest and most famous, but women's music festivals sprang up throughout the United States and Canada. Musicians such as Holly Near, Meg Christian, Chris Williamson, Maxine Feldman, Alix Dobkin, and the group Sweet Honey in the Rock traveled all over to give lesbians musical expression and community. And the first women's music recording label, Olivia Records, was created by a collective of women in 1973.

This 2015 photo portrays Chirlane McCray, one of the women who was involved in the Combahee River Women's Collective, a lesbian commune that existed in the 1970s.

Many lesbians also established lesbian separatist collective family homes, the first of which was called the Furies (1971–1973), after the Greek goddesses of vengeance. There, Rita Mae Brown, Charlotte Bunch, Joan Biren, and others sought to create a haven away from negative patriarchal influences. Another collective was the Combahee River Collective (1974–1980), whose members, including Barbara Smith, Eleanor Johnson, Chirlane McCray, and Audre Lorde, became the most famous originators of black lesbian feminism. Black lesbian feminism is geared toward assisting black lesbians and helping others understand the social needs of black lesbians.

Lesbians also founded women's community centers, homeless and domestic violence shelters, collective farms (often organic), schools, and vocational programs.

CHAPTER FIVE

CREATING SPACES AND CHANGING INSTITUTIONS

W hile lesbians were liberating themselves from misogyny and patriarchy, transgender women and effeminate gay men also began to organize separately. They had to because lesbians and noneffeminate men discriminated against them. It was on the backdrop of these attempts at organizing that the LGBTQ+ community succeeded in a massive institutional undertaking.

ANTITRANS ATTITUDES AMONG GAY MEN AND LESBIANS

The wider gay liberation movement often looked down upon effeminate gay street hustlers, drag queens, and transvestites. Many lesbians did not like drag queens because they felt that drag performances (both commercial and informal) mocked the very real difficulties faced by women who sought to escape the rigid gender roles (and clothes, shoes, manners, and duties) that men had historically created for women. High heels damaged feet, makeup marred skin, and being limited

In 1975, Wayne County, a musician and drag performer, sang at Eros 75, a gay club in New York City. She later changed her stage name to Jayne County.

to household duties demeaned them, but men considered women to be at a disadvantage when they didn't fit into that mold. Men had controlled, discriminated against, and violently harmed women for thousands of years, and by this point, many women—lesbian and nonlesbian alike—had had enough of it. They thus felt that the exaggerated speech patterns, costumes, wigs, and behavior of drag queens and transvestites (who would later be referred to as transgender and transsexual) unsettling and demeaning to women.

Many lesbians also felt that effeminate male drag queens and transvestites were mocking the actions and sacrifices women had made in the movement to further gay liberation by insisting that they had started the movement. After all, butch lesbians were notable at the Stonewall riots, and lesbians had helped create the GLF and the commemorative marches.

Gay men also had negative attitudes toward transgender women. Marsha P. Johnson expressed the sense of distaste that gay men had toward her and other women:

> We still feel oppression by other gay brothers.
> Gay sisters don't think too bad of transvestites.
> Gay brothers do. I went to a dance at Gay
> Activist Alliance last week, and there was not
> even one gay brother that came over and
> said hello…Once in a while, I get an invitation
> to Daughters of Bilitis, and when I go there,

they're always warm. All the gay sisters come over and say, "Hello, we're glad to see you," and they start long conversations…A lot of gay brothers don't like women! And transvestites remind you of women. A lot of gay brothers don't feel too close to women, they'd rather be near men, that's how come they're gay.

STREET TRANSVESTITES ACTION REVOLUTIONARIES

The attitude that transgender people faced from both gay men and women alike might have pushed them out of the gay liberation movement if they weren't so self-determined. However, Johnson and Sylvia Rivera began a group called Street Transvestites Action Revolutionaries (STAR). Rivera said of starting STAR, "We formed STAR because my brothers and sisters kept using us when they needed us, but they weren't treating us fairly…It was not even the men that pushed aside the drag queens. It was the gay women from this radical group."

STAR was a collective that housed and protected homeless effeminate youth, especially black and Hispanic youth who were among the most vulnerable in New York City's street community. They staged a zap at New York University in 1971 but were unsuccessful in obtaining much support from the rest of the gay and lesbian community. They were summarily arrested.

Marsha P. Johnson, shown here in an advertisement for a Netflix feature about her life, helped form STAR to assist New York City's homeless drag queens, transvestites, and transsexual people.

STAR lasted only a couple of years, partly because of the tenuous existence of the participants. They were often in and out of jail and didn't have secure, long-term housing. However, STAR represented the first organization begun by and for drag queens, transvestites, and transsexual people. Eventually, small underground social clubs in many cities were formed by MTF (male to female) transvestites and transsexual people as a way to achieve social connections and as safe places to wear women's clothes. Eventually, organizations for FTMs (females-to-males) were founded, such as FTM International in 1986. There were also organizations devoted to obtaining legal and political rights and freedom from social stigma for transgender and gender-nonconforming people. Some were the Sylvia Rivera Law Project, started in 2002 and named in Rivera's honor, and the Transgender Legal Defense and Education Fund, started in 2003.

STUDENT ACTIVISM

College students were also affected by the Stonewall riots. There were only a couple of gay-oriented student groups before 1969, but many began to found gay student alliances at universities. Both GLF and GAA were influential in this task. Gary Pavlic, one of the founders of the University at Albany Gay and Lesbian Alliance (now Pride Alliance) and the Albany region Gay Community Center (now Pride Center), stated:

Things were happening, Stonewall had just happened in '69. Things were starting to move in the community; we were getting very active in Albany at the time. There was nothing at a major university center. [...] I got what is now

(continued on the next page)

(continued from the previous page)

the Pride Alliance up and running, it was [called] the Gay and Lesbian Alliance at that time. I got it started in 1970, and it's been functioning ever since. I did start it, if you go to the University at Albany and look at their papers, my name is as the first Chairman. [...] So, it kept going through my mind, if not me, who, if not here, where, if not now, when.

Colleges throughout the country also started offering gay studies courses, women's studies courses, and even some gay and lesbian studies departments and women's studies departments. Jack Collins established the first Department of Gay and Lesbian Studies in the United States after teaching gay literature in 1972. John De Cecco established a center for sexuality studies at San Francisco State University.

FIGHTING THE STIGMA OF MENTAL ILLNESS

Just as Reverend Perry's campaign to give gay men and lesbians a spiritual home began before the Stonewall riots, the search for recognition within the mental health profession that homosexuals were mentally sane also began before Stonewall. Frank Kameny and Barbara Gittings of the Daughters of Bilitis had written to many psychiatrists. Their

Gay rights activist Frank Kameny (*right*) appears with President Barack Obama in 2009 during a signing ceremony for a presidential memorandum giving benefits to same-sex spouses of federal employees.

group and the Mattachine Society had allowed many psychiatrists to visit their meetings, but this would offer nothing more than disappointment. These psychiatrists and psychologists only recommended ways to cure homosexuality.

However, there was some hope. A small organization within the American Psychiatric Association (APA) called GayPA for gay and lesbian psychiatrists had begun to meet secretly and only with other closeted queer APA members to exchange support. They were in a unique position of influence that might impact their community positively, but they also faced the risk of losing that position if found out.

Frank Kameny, who had been campaigning against the federal government to get his job back since he lost it due to his sexuality in 1957, felt that through continued exposure psychiatrists would eventually come to declare homosexuality normal. But after 1969, he and others felt the matter was more urgent than the amount of time continued exposure would require. In 1965, Kameny had written, "The most important single issue facing our movement today, [is] the proclamation of homosexual sanity."

THE CAMPAIGN AGAINST THE AMERICAN PSYCHIATRIC ASSOCIATION

The gay liberation movement was now ready to take on a behemoth: it was time to organize a more fervent campaign to change the official psychiatric diagnosis of homosexuals as "mentally sick" and "abnormal."

In 1970, a rowdy zap by the GLF convinced the APA to allow a panel at their 1971 conference. At this conference, Kameny, Gittings, and Jack Baker spoke on behalf of the GLF.

The Mattachine Society, the Gay Activists Alliance, and the Gay Liberation Front had also organized a zap during Surgeon General Ramsay Clark's convocation speech. The action devolved into a physical battle between psychiatrists and activists. In spite of the rough response, the attention garnered enough support from the APA to allow Gittings to spearhead the creation of an exhibit, Gay, Proud, and Healthy: The Homosexual Community Speaks.

The next year, several serendipitous meetings between Ronald Gold, the media director of the New York GAA, and Dr. Robert Spitzer, a member of the APA's Nomenclature Committee, led to a gradual understanding that there should be an open debate about getting rid of the designation of homosexuality as a disease in the DSM. Spitzer and Gold drafted a resolution to the APA requesting that homosexuality be removed from the DSM, and Spitzer and Kameny drafted a "justifying letter" to the Nomenclature Committee.

Finally, in December 1973, the committee voted to remove homosexuality from the list of psychosexual disorders in the DSM. However, many psychiatrists were unconvinced, so they campaigned hard against these changes. The decision was left to a mail-in ballot vote that all APA members could participate in in 1974. With a final tally of 58 percent of members upholding the decision, the APA membership voted to retain the committee's decision and exclude homosexuality from the disorders list. Finally, it was canon: gay men and lesbians were not sick, mentally deranged, or abnormal.

This photo shows the fifth edition of the *DSM-5* reference book. The first *Diagnostic and Statistical Manual of Mental Disorders* was published in 1952.

This decision was every bit as important as Kameny had predicted. It finally gave gay men and lesbians the ability to demand from the law the same rights as the medical profession had given them: they should no longer be imprisoned for being homosexual because there was, in fact, nothing wrong with them and they should not be treated like criminals.

However, it shouldn't be ignored that editions of the *DSM-II* and *DSM-III* did include sexual orientation disturbance (SOD) and ego dystonic homosexuality (EDH), respectively. These were both essentially the same thing: a diagnosis of a sexual orientation that is disturbing to one who holds the identity and a sufficient ailment to justify the survival of conversion therapy. It wouldn't be until 1987, in the *DSM-III-R*, that all references to homosexuality as a psychological disorder would be eradicated.

As of March 2018, further work remains to be done for the validation of transgender and cross-dressing identities, since *DSM-5* still lists classifications for both of these categories.

CHAPTER SIX

CONSERVATIVE BACKLASH TAKES THE NATIONAL STAGE

The conservative backlash against gay liberation efforts offers a clear image of the obstacles LGBTQ+ people have faced. Anita Bryant's Save Our Children Campaign was one such effort. It began as an attempt to repeal an antidiscrimination bill in Dade County, Florida, and ended up becoming a model for similar antigay political and social campaigns all over the United States. This battle came to symbolize the legal canonization of hate toward LGBTQ+ people and made the LGBTQ+ activist community realize that its work would not be easy or quick.

ANTIDISCRIMINATION IN DADE COUNTY

The gay liberation movement's push for more social and political equality with heterosexual people was met with widespread and organized antigay and antilesbian campaigns in response. Politicians, celebrities, powerful lobby groups, and grassroots campaigns joined together as never before to oppose the advances made socially and legally by gay and lesbian groups.

The stakes were clear. Conservative heterosexuals had heretofore assumed an uncomplicated superiority over lesbian and gay people and only begrudgingly responded to changing circumstances.

In the late 1970s, two campaigns launched by conservatives had a profound effect on both gays and lesbians and conservative heterosexuals. The beginning of the so-called religious right came in 1977 in Dade County, Florida. In that year, the group Dade County Coalition for the Humanistic Rights of

Anita Bryant, Christian singer and political activist, talks to reporters on June 7, 1977, about her successful efforts to repeal the Dade County Gay Rights Referendum.

Gays (CHRG) managed, after much lobbying, to get a somewhat limited nondiscrimination ordinance on the table.

Many people in Miami were shocked, particularly at the Southern Baptist church that Anita Bryant attended. As Bryant explained, "As a concerned mother of four children—ages 13 to 8 years—I am most definitely against this ordinance amendment because you would be discriminating against my children's right to grow up in a healthy, decent community." Bryant's church, Northwest Baptist, and its pastor, Reverend William Chapman, were also horrified by the idea of gay people being afforded any civil rights.

The ordinance narrowly passed, five to three, after several hours of intense testimony.

SODOMY LAWS

The term "sodomy" comes from a biblical story that occurs in a place called Sodom. As the story goes, several male residents wanted to sexually assault two male angels who were visiting Abraham's nephew Lot. However, Lot managed to save the angels from being raped. Because of this attempted attack, God destroyed the town by fire and earthquake after allowing Lot and most of his family to escape.

Society would attempt to perpetuate this violence against queers, as if it were logical to equate rape with consensual sexual activity, and to state that the existence of queer people, per se, prevented them from teaching lessons of morality within their families. In the late nineteenth and early twentieth centuries, every state passed sodomy laws. They declared that all forms of homosexual sex and heterosexual, nonprocreative sex (sometimes regardless of whether it occurred in marriage or outside), were crimes. Every state didn't ban all of these activities, though.

By the 1950s, men could be arrested for things as simple as hugs as well as for more overt flirting with police officers who meant to entrap them. Lesbians were more likely to be convicted for lewdness; sodomy laws were more often enforced against gay men.

A sodomy conviction meant a prison sentence, and it ruined careers and families. Many people committed suicide when their names were published in local papers after an arrest for sodomy or a lewd act.

Homophile groups fought earnestly against rampant police entrapment and sodomy laws. As early as 1962, Illinois was the first state to rescind its sodomy laws. One tactic commonly used after the Stonewall riots was suing the government and demanding change via the state supreme court. By 1980, many states had decriminalized sodomy in some way, including Connecticut (1971), Colorado (1972), California (1976), Delaware (1973), Massachusetts (1974), Iowa (1978), and Ohio (1974).

THE SAVE OUR CHILDREN CAMPAIGN IS BORN

In the days immediately after the Dade County ordinance was passed, Reverend Chapman and Robert Brake, a local Catholic attorney, encouraged Anita Bryant to create a campaign against this ordinance. Encouraging Bryant, in particular, couldn't have been purely coincidental. Bryant was nationally known as a singer of very popular songs, such as "Till There Was You" and "Paper Roses." She was an actor and did ads for Singer sewing machines, Kraft Foods, Coca-Cola, and the Florida Citrus Commission. Her platform would make her a formidable opponent.

Bryant's campaign was called Save Our Children (SOC). Bryant felt that she was doing God's work. She led large prayer rallies and worked with a broad coalition of religious groups and other people against the ordinance. Large ads were bought and placed in local papers to rally support. They vigorously collected signatures to petition Dade County to repeal the ordinance.

Alan Rockway (*left*) and Doris Dennis (*right*) hand out literature against and for, respectively, the repeal of the Dade County Gay Rights Referendum in 1977.

Reverend Jack Wyrtzen, a pastor who had formed the Word of Life Ministries, also helped stir antigay furor. He said, "If this bill passes in Dade County in favor of the gay crowd, it could be the end of the United States of America."

Through their aggressive media campaign, they were eventually able to collect 64,304 signatures.

The campaign was enlarged to become an anti–gay rights organization working across America and elicited heated responses both from politically conservative and liberal people across the nation. The antigay movement arose shortly after the gay liberation movement itself was born. It was a response to the perceived increase in attacks on what conservatives considered "normal" society and sexuality.

UNITY DEFEATS DISHARMONY

The CHRG was blindsided by this flurry of antigay activity. They quickly realized that this campaign would escalate into a national antigay campaign and that they should prepare a national campaign against SOC. CHRG cofounder Bob Basker said, "It will send ripples across the country either way. If this is defeated we are looking at a witch hunt against the gays."

The coalition changed its name to Dade County Coalition for Human Rights (CHR) and began to create a more measured strategy. But building membership proved to be difficult because large numbers of gay people were not willing to get involved politically in the movement. Many simply wanted to live their lives and not attract more negative attention. The coalition was also split between the differing visions of its leaders. Disagreement hinged partially on whether to use militant or conservative tactics. This caused the coalition to have a hard time committing to actions.

CHR decided to boycott Florida orange juice. This particularly central tactic quickly spread through the nation. Gay men and lesbians in New York, California, and states in between created their own

Many gay men and lesbians boycotted orange juice that the Florida Citrus Commission promoted in hopes of putting pressure on the growers to drop Anita Bryant as spokesperson.

Coalitions for Human Rights and their own local boycotts of Florida orange juice. However, in spite of its efforts, the coalition was at no point able to wage an adequate campaign against SOC, whose tactics and solid voting bloc were far more tangible. As a result, Dade County voters repealed the 1977 antidiscrimination ordinance.

THE TURNING TIDES OF GAY LIBERATION

Anita Bryant's national brand-name status, her financial backing, and her organizationally astute copartners were eager to capitalize on the repeal of the Dade County antidiscrimination ordinance. They began campaigning against similar ordinances in other cities. Bryant's Save Our Children campaign— later renamed Protect America's Children—would increase in size and strength.

Bryant and other antigay people established similar campaigns in cities across America. These campaigns even inspired direct violence against gay men and lesbians. San Franciscan Robert Hillsborough was murdered by men allegedly chanting, "This is for Anita!" Several fires were set, and muggings and other murders were committed in San Francisco in the summer and fall of 1977.

By 1978, the gay liberation movement had reached a stalemate with the conservatives, and in some ways, the tide began to turn against them. As more cities enacted antidiscrimination bills, conservatives relied on propaganda tactics to drive voters toward them and against gay men and lesbians. This new, fierce conservative backlash spurred the LGBTQ+ community to commit to a renewed effort to recapture and consolidate the gains they had achieved since 1969.

But any chance at winning the battles that loomed would require a more strategic approach. One lesson they could take from the ordinance repeal was evaluating the success of their tactics. The best coalition tactic, the orange juice boycott, didn't work well largely because the Florida Citrus Commission refused to be persuaded by the boycotters' financial incentive—they were only able to take away an insignificant quantity of sales. Even if the commission fired Bryant, that wouldn't necessarily translate to political action happening in Dade County, or anywhere else, to prevent antigay discrimination. However, the Florida Citrus Commission did fire Bryant in 1978, suggesting that the protest made the commission reconsider how they positioned themselves to their customers.

CHAPTER SEVEN

THE END OF AN ERA

I n the midst of backlash throughout this era,
there were also gay and lesbian politicians. They
would not only win office, but they would also
make significant contributions to progress in and
out of office. The national march on Washington
would serve as a depiction of the culmination of
the new, undeniable status of gay politics and
as a symbol of all that had been gained in the
aftermath of Stonewall.

ELAINE NOBLE'S ACCOMPLISHMENTS AND FAILURES

One of the ways that gay men and lesbians began
to fight back against antigay forces in society was
by creating voting blocs that would elect openly
gay and lesbian officials. Representation meant
not only the ability to influence the government,
but also gaining a better understanding of how the
government ran.

Elaine Noble addresses the crowd at a 1977 gay rights rally on Boston Common. She served as the first openly gay state representative between 1975 and 1979.

In the mid- and late 1970s, more and more gay and lesbian people ran to be elected into government offices, both local and statewide. Elaine Noble was the first out gay person to be elected to a state legislative position; she was elected in 1975 to the Massachusetts State House of Representatives. During the campaign, her home was vandalized, her car was sabotaged, and her supporters were harassed. She also received death threats, and those didn't end after she won the election.

She tried to get an antidiscrimination bill passed, but it didn't get enough support. In March 1977, she was chosen to meet with President Jimmy Carter to discuss issues concerning the LGBTQ+ community. In 1978, she unsuccessfully ran for US Senate and ended up working for Kevin White, the mayor of Boston. She was also unsuccessful in a 1990s election for a city council position in Cambridge, Massachusetts.

After exiting politics, she went on to cofound a rehabilitation center in Minneapolis called the Pride Institute. This institution serves LGBTQ+ clients as they attempt to recover from substance abuse and improve their mental and sexual health.

THE "NO ON 6" CAMPAIGN

One particularly well-known gay politician was the late Harvey Milk. He grew up in New York but eventually went to San Francisco to be in a more gay-friendly community. He decided to campaign to be on the city's board of supervisors in 1973 and 1975, but he lost both times. In 1976, he ran for state assembly but lost then, too. Finally, in November 1977, he was elected to the San Francisco City-County Board, largely because San Francisco changed the process from a citywide election to district blocs. Milk was elected from District 5, which contained the mostly gay Castro district.

Milk, who was the target of vandalism and death threats early on, realized that he would probably be killed. Unusually, he tape-recorded a will and his thoughts about what it meant for him to be an out politician: "Let the bullets that rip through my brain smash through every closet door in the nation."

One of the primary projects that Harvey Milk worked on was the "NO on 6" campaign. Partly because of Anita Bryant's success through her Save Our Children campaign, State Senator John Briggs sponsored a bill, Proposition 6, that would have allowed the firing of anyone employed in California public schools who was involved in "advocating, imposing, encouraging or promoting" homosexual activity. That bill implicated gay men, lesbians, and their supporters, and it was also known as the Briggs Initiative.

Having learned from the failed Dade County Coalition campaign, Milk, Tom Ammiano (who would later become the president of the San Francisco Board of Supervisors), Sally Gearhart, David Mixner, Peter Scott, and others organized a campaign against the Briggs Initiative. Milk founded the group San Franciscans Against Proposition 6, and other activists formed the Bay Area Committee Against the Briggs Initiative (BACABI). Milk and Gearhart held prominent debates about the initiative.

Each group had its own tactics. Milk's group held debates, organized phone banking, and

City Supervisor Harvey Milk (*left*) shakes hands with San Francisco mayor George Moscone in 1978. Milk was the first openly gay elected official in California and helped to pass a gay rights ordinance.

ran ads in the media, while the BACABI used speakers in a grassroots effort to reach voters from town to town. After Mixner and Scott had a meeting with Governor Ronald Reagan, Reagan began to oppose Proposition 6. This was a huge factor in the opinions of many voters. On November 7, 1978, the result was clear: 58.4 percent voted no, and 41.6 percent voted yes. Preventing Proposition 6 from being passed was an important win during a difficult time for gay rights activists.

HARVEY MILK'S DEATH

During that year, Milk had developed a tempestuous relationship with Dan White, one of the other city supervisors. White

Harvey Milk's body was taken out of San Francisco City Hall on November 21, 1978, after former city supervisor Dan White shot and killed Milk and Mayor Moscone.

was not particularly gay friendly, but he found he had some things in common with Milk.

White grew to resent Milk because it seemed that Milk got more support in getting his city ordinances and bills passed than did White. Eventually he decided to resign as a supervisor, but after having a change of heart, he asked Mayor George Moscone for reinstatement. Moscone's answer was no.

On November 21, 1978, White went into city hall and shot and killed Moscone and Milk. This was shocking to the entire city. Acting mayor Dianne Feinstein announced the news

THE NATIONAL MARCH ON WASHINGTON

Many people, including comedian Robin Tyler, had called for a march in 1979 to honor Stonewall. Tyler and several others attempted to organize a march from the St. Paul base of their gay rights group, but internal problems meant that they would not complete the task. Milk, who had become a trusted and iconic politician for gay men and lesbians across America, asked Harry Britt to organize one.

Britt, along with Bruce Voeller and Jean O'Leary of the National Gay Task Force, created a National Outreach Committee and began the arduous task of organizing disparate people from various parts of the country. After Milk's death, the planning proceeded with more haste and dynamism. The will to demonstrate to the country the size and strength of the gay community was immense. Steve Ault of the New York Coalition for Lesbian and Gay Rights became the lead

At the October 14, 1979, National March on Washington for Lesbian and Gay Rights, thousands of gay men and lesbians marched in Washington, DC, to obtain recognition, equality, and civil rights.

(continued on the next page)

(continued from the previous page)

coordinator, and Reverend Perry and Tyler would head up the march with what was called a Gay Freedom Train, meant to both pick up participants and lead rallies in support of the march. The date for the National March on Washington for Lesbian and Gay Rights was set for October 14, 1979.

The march had thousands of participants; contingents from cities, towns, and organizations across America came. There were veterans, teachers, doctors, and every type of profession, class, and race, and they were all there to show support to the LGBTQ+ community. Mothers and fathers and relatives of gay men and lesbians came and marched.

The march was a great success, and people began to look forward to the development of a more concerted national consciousness about the rights of gay men and lesbians. The march was also symbolic of a bolder effort by queer people to secure their civil rights and be acknowledged in their right to exist and be accepted by society.

tearfully. Gay men and lesbians marched up to city hall from the Castro district and held a vigil that night. Milk had become a martyr for gay rights.

White was acquitted of first-degree murder due to the "Twinkie defense," claiming that the loss of his job combined with his unhealthy eating habits had deepened his depression and a depressed person was incapable of planning a murder in advance. He was thus only convicted of voluntary manslaughter and sentenced to a mere seven years and eight months in prison, of which he served only five years. On May 21, 1979, the night of the sentencing, the Castro district erupted in the White Night riots, in which more than five thousand people damaged the San Francisco City Hall building and set fire to several police cars. The police responded with a raid on a local gay bar, the Elephant Walk, and officers began fighting with gay people in the streets in a conflict that lasted two hours.

THE ROAD AHEAD

As the decade ended, many were exhilarated at the triumphs of the LGBTQ+ community. There had been hard-won victories, and the difficulties—legal, political, and social—had been enormous. Not only had conservatives tried to destroy the gains made, but the gay and lesbian community itself had fractured into various segments: gay men, lesbians (and lesbian separatists), drag queens and transvestites, working and middle classes, the old homophile stalwarts, and the young new militants. Despite frequent disagreements, each group contributed vastly to the gay liberation movement, and when united, they often provoked incredible change.

In the 1980s, renewed conservative backlash would emerge as much of the nation collectively rebelled against the liberal nature of the 1960s and 1970s. In addition, the emergence of acquired immunodeficiency syndrome, or AIDS (originally called gay-related immune deficiency, or GRID), would devastate gay male populations and forever change the landscape of activism that arose in the 1970s. The 1980s would see further agitation, largely on behalf of AIDS patients, with organizations like AIDS Coalition to Unleash Power, or ACT UP. The 1980s would also see the beginnings of a global gay and lesbian rights movement and a worldwide dialogue on what it means to be gay, which have survived to the contemporary era. The message this continued movement sends is clear: as long as there are rights to be won in the pursuit of equality, there will be activists working toward making that equality a reality.

TIMELINE

1966 Compton's Cafeteria riot happens in San Francisco's Tenderloin district.

1967 The Black Cat Tavern riot occurs in Los Angeles.

1969 On June 28, the Stonewall riots begin in New York City.

The Gay Liberation Front is founded on July 24.

In November, the Gay Activists Alliance is founded.

1970 In May, a group called Radicalesbians, consisting of Karla Jay and Rita Mae Brown among others, interrupts the NOW Second Congress to Unite Women to read their manifesto "The Woman-Identified Woman" as a means of empowering women during the lavender scare.

In June, the first Christopher Street Gay Liberation March occurs.

1973 The American Psychiatric Association formally drops homosexuality, per se, as a disease from the *Diagnostic and Statistical Manual of Mental Disorders*.

1975 Elaine Noble, who is openly gay, is elected to the Massachusetts House of Representatives.

1976 The first Michigan Womyn's music festival occurs.

1977 On January 18, Dade County, Florida, passes an antidiscrimination bill that impacts the LGBTQ+ community.

The Save Our Children campaign, led by Anita Bryant, successfully passes an ordinance that repealed the nondiscrimination bill by a vote of 69.3–39.6 percent on June 7.

Harvey Milk is elected as a city supervisor on November 8.

1978 Rev. Troy Perry founds the Metropolitan Community Church on October 6.

California's Proposition 6 (Briggs Initiative) is defeated on November 7, after Harvey Milk's successful campaign against it.

Harvey Milk is assassinated on November 27.

1979 The National March on Washington for Lesbian and Gay Rights occurs.

GLOSSARY

boycott To refuse to support a business or institution for political reasons.

butch Originally, an aggressive young man, but currently used to mean a masculine lesbian.

campaign A concerted effort by citizens and politicians to achieve a stated and clear-cut objective, such as to elect a candidate or to get antidiscrimination laws passed.

canon A widely accepted set of professional, religious, educational, or social standards of a period; canonized standards are often controversial because they might unfairly exclude or disparage some people or ideas.

discrimination An action that overtly favors one group or person over another.

drag queen A man who dresses in women's clothing and accessories and performs comedic acts in the guise of a woman.

femme A feminine lesbian.

galvanize To convince someone in a shocking manner to do something.

heterosexual Someone who loves or has sex with someone of the opposite sex.

homophile A person who loves or is sexually attracted to someone of the same sex or gender.

homosexual A person who is sexually attracted and/or romantically attracted to someone of the same sex.

misogyny A belief that women are morally,

intellectually, spiritually, and physically inferior to men.

patriarchy A culture in which men legally retain the majority of power in society, in which family structures support male inheritance over female inheritance, or in which men dominate women and children.

queen A slang term for an effeminate gay man.

second-wave feminism A feminist movement from the 1960s and 1980s that emphasized issues concerning gender-based violence, family, the workplace, and other problematic areas of women's lives. This movement was criticized for not considering and addressing the needs of women of color.

separatist Someone who wishes to be separate from another group he or she finds troubling, annoying, or damaging.

sodomy laws Laws that originally forbade oral and anal sex between couples of the opposite sex and same sex. They were enforced primarily against gay men in the twentieth century.

transvestite A person who dresses in clothing typically associated with a gender that doesn't match that person's identify; a cross-dresser.

zap A public rally, dispersion of literature, march, protest, or some other action that gay activists organized to garner public attention to their plight and their demands.

FOR MORE INFORMATION

The Ali Forney Center (AFC)
321 West 125th Street
New York, NY 10027
(212) 206-0574
Website: http://www.aliforneycenter.org
Facebook: @AliForney
Twitter: @AliForneyCenter
The AFC is the largest organization in the United
    States dedicated to providing resources,
    including housing, job preparedness, and
    health care services, for LGBTQ+ youth who
    are homeless.

Canadian Centre for Gender & Sexual Diversity
440 Albert Street, Suite C304
Albert Street Educational Centre
Ottawa, ON K1R 5B5
Canada
(613) 400-1875
Website: http://ccgsd-ccdgs.org
Facebook and Twitter: @ccgsd.ccdgs
This center runs programs in the United States and
    Canada that are meant to prevent discrimination
    and bullying and heal transgender and
    nonheterosexual victims.

Community One Foundation
PO Box 760 – Station F
Toronto, ON M4Y 2N6
Canada

(416) 920-5422
Website: http://communityone.ca
Facebook: @CommunityOneFoundation
Twitter: @C1Foundation
Instagram: @c1foundation
This foundation offers financial support to
developing LGBTQ+ communities in Toronto.

Gay and Lesbian Alliance Against Defamation
(GLAAD)
104 West 29th Street, #4
New York, NY 10001
(212) 629-3322
Website: http://glaad.org
Facebook and Twitter: @glaad
Founded in 1985, this organization seeks to
correct the media coverage of LGBTQ+ people
and to award outstanding LGBTQ+ media
activists and allies.

GLSEN
110 William Street, 30th Floor
New York, NY 10038
(212) 727-0135
Website: https://www.glsen.org
Facebook and Twitter: @GLSEN
This organization offers academic, legal, and
administrative resources to students and
teachers and conducts research regarding
the treatment and needs of LGBTQ+ K–12
students.

Harvey Milk Foundation
PO Box 5666
Fort Lauderdale, FL 33310
(954) 240-8819
Website: http://milkfoundation.org
Facebook: @Harvey.Milk.Foundation
This foundation encourages and creates school
   curricula based on Harvey Milk's achievements
   and promotes LGBTQ+ equality globally.

Human Rights Campaign
1640 Rhode Island Avenue NW
Washington, DC 20036-3278
(202) 628-4160
Website: http://www.hrc.org
Twitter: @hrc
Facebook: @humanrightscampaign
Instagram: @HumanRightsCampaign
The HRC is a political action committee that is
   devoted to supporting pro-LGBTQ+ political
   candidates. It also conducts research and
   advocacy for LGBTQ+ rights and lobbies
   Congress and other governing groups to promote
   LGBTQ+ equality bills.

Metropolitan Community Church (MCC)
PO Box 50488
Sarasota, FL 34232
(310) 360-8640
Website: http://mccchurch.org
Facebook and Twitter: @MCCchurch

This Protestant church was founded to allow gay men and lesbians to attend and participate openly. The church's leadership and membership remains primarily LGBTQ+, and the church gets involved in LGBTQ+ activism.

National Center for Lesbian Rights
870 Market Street, Suite 370
San Francisco, CA 94102
(415) 392-6257
Website: http://www.nclrights.org
Facebook: @nclrights
Founded in 1977, this center is a nonprofit law firm that assists in all sorts of legal cases for all LGBTQ+ people, although it originally served lesbians exclusively. It takes cases related to same-sex marriage, imprisonment, adoption, employment, discrimination, immigration, and various other topics.

Sylvia Rivera Law Project (SRLP)
147 W 24th Street, 5th Floor
New York, NY 10011
(212) 337-8550
Website: https://srlp.org/about/contact
Facebook: @SylviaRiveraLawProject
Twitter: @SRLP
The Sylvia Rivera Law Project works to guarantee the rights of all people to self-determine their gender identity and expression and to live lives free from harassment, discrimination, and violence, regardless of race and class.

FOR FURTHER READING

Bausum, Ann. *Stonewall: Breaking Out in the Fight for Gay Rights*. New York, NY: Penguin, 2016.

Brettschneider, Marla, Susan Burgess, and Christine Keating, eds. *LGBTQ Politics: A Critical Reader*. New York, NY: New York University Press, 2017.

Goldberg, Abbie E. *The Sage Encyclopedia of LGBTQ Studies*. Thousand Oaks, CA: Sage, 2016.

Grinapol, Corinne. *Harvey Milk: Pioneering Gay Politician*. New York, NY: Rosen Publishing, 2015.

Henneberg, Susan. *James Baldwin: Groundbreaking Author and Civil Rights Activist* (Remarkable LGBTQ Lives). New York, NY: Rosen Publishing, 2015.

Mardell, Ashley. *The ABC's of LGBT: Helping You Become the Best You*. Miami, FL: Mango Media, 2016.

Oldham, Victoria. *Late Outbursts: LGBTQ Memoirs*. Nottingham, UK: Global Words Press, 2014.

Pohlen, Jerome. *Gay & Lesbian History for Kids: The Century Long Struggle for LGBT Rights, with 21 Activities*. Chicago, IL: Chicago Review Press, 2016.

Rodi, Robert, and Laura Ross. *Understanding Sexual Orientation and Gender Identity*. Broomall, PA: Mason Crest, 2017.

Stevenson, Robin. *Pride: Celebrating Diversity & Community*. Victoria, CA: Orca Book Publishers, 2016.

BIBLIOGRAPHY

American Psychiatric Association. *Diagnostic and Statistical Manual: Mental Disorders*. Washington, DC: American Psychiatric Association, 1952.

Bronski, Michael. *A Queer History of the United States*. Boston, MA: Beacon Press, 2011.

Cain, Paul D. "Interview: David Carter: Historian of the Stonewall Riots." GayToday.com, July 1, 2004. http://gaytoday.com/interview/070104in.asp.

Carter, David. *Stonewall: The Riots That Sparked the Gay Revolution*. New York, NY: St. Martin's Griffin, 2005.

Christian, Paula. *Edge of Twilight*. Greenwich, CT: Fawcett Publications, 1961.

Combahee River Collective. "Black Feminist Statement." Graduate Center, CUNY, April 1977. https://wgs10016.commons.gc.cuny.edu/combahee-river-collective-black-feminist-statement.

Davis, Kate, and David Heilbroner. *Stonewall Uprising*. PBS *American Experience*, 2010. Film.

Duberman, Martin B. *Stonewall*. New York, NY: Plume, 1994.

Dynes, Wayne R. *Encyclopedia of Homosexuality, Vol. 1*. Abingdon, UK: Routledge, 2016.

Emmerich, Roland, dir. *Stonewall*. 2009; Centropolis Entertainment/MELS, Film.

Faderman, Lillian. *The Gay Revolution: The Story of the Struggle*. New York, NY: Simon & Schuster, 2015.

Faderman, Lillian, and Stuart Timmons. *Gay L.A:*

A History of Sexual Outlaws, Power Politics, and Lipstick Lesbians. Berkeley, CA: University of California Press, 2009.

Lisker, Jerry. "Homo Nest Raided, Queen Bees Are Stinging Mad." Reprinted from the *New York Daily News*, July 6, 1969. http://www.cs.cmu .edu/afs/cs/user/scotts/ftp/bulgarians/NY-DN _Stonewall.txt.

Marcus, Eric. *Making History: The Struggle for Gay and Lesbian Equal Rights 1945–1990*. New York, NY: Harper Collins, 1992.

Priest, James C. *Private School*. New York, NY: Universal Publishing and Distributing, 1959.

Radicalesbians. "A Woman-Identified Woman," 1970. https://wgs10016.commons.gc.cuny .edu/radicalesbians-the-woman-identified -woman.

Smith, Artemis. *The Third Sex*. New York, NY: Universal, 1959.

Stryker, Susan, and Buskirk J. Van. *Gay by the Bay: A History of Queer Culture in the San Francisco Bay Area*. San Francisco, CA: Chronicle Books, 1996.

Teal, Donn. *The Gay Militants*. New York, NY: St. Martin's Press, 1995.

Zimmerman, Bonnie. *Encyclopedia of Lesbian Histories and Cultures*. Abingdon, UK: Routledge, 2014.

INDEX

A

American Psychiatric
    Association (APA), 69–71,
    73
antidiscrimination bill, 52,
    82–83, 86
    Dade County, 74–76, 82

B

bars, 6, 21, 22, 27, 31, 32,
    33, 35, 37–38, 43, 46
    raids on, 22–23, 25, 28,
    30, 46, 95
Black Cat Tavern riot, 6, 22,
    24–25, 27
boycott, of orange juice,
    81–82, 83
Brown, Rita Mae, 55,
    57–58, 61
Bryant, Anita, 74, 76, 78, 82,
    83, 87
butch lesbians, 23, 27–28,
    30, 33, 64

C

Castro district, 86–87, 94, 95
civil rights movement, 6–7,

13, 40
    for gays and lesbians, 24,
    53, 76, 94
Coalition for the Humanistic
    Rights of Gays (CHRG),
    75–76, 80
Compton's Cafeteria riot,
    24–25, 27
conservative backlash, to gay
    movement, 74, 75, 76,
    78, 80, 81, 82–83, 95, 96
conversion therapy, 17, 73

D

Daughters of Bilitis (DOB),
    19, 21–22, 42, 64–65, 68
*Diagnostic and Statistical
    Manual, The*, 17, 71, 73
discrimination, against gay
    men and lesbians, 9, 11,
    13, 14, 36, 46, 53, 62, 64
drag queens, 23, 24–25,
    27–28, 32, 33, 34, 42,
    43, 62, 64, 65, 66, 95

F

feminism
    black lesbian, 58–59, 71
    lesbian, 52–53, 55

ABOUT THE AUTHOR

Dr. Sean Heather K. McGraw is an independent scholar and former adjunct lecturer at various institutions, including the University at Albany and Siena College. She has also been a librarian and national park guide. She is writing a book about the Albany LGBTQ+ community and also conducting further research based on her earlier work "Striving for Salvation: Margaret Anna Cusack, Sainthood, Religious Foundations and Revolution in Ireland 1830–1900." She also enjoys stage acting, playing the harp, and storytelling.

PHOTO CREDITS